Thorns & Roses

Glicia De Almeida

BookLeaf
Publishing

Presentation by *BookLeaf Publishing*

Web: www.bookleafpub.com

E-mail: info@bookleafpub.com

ISBN: 9789357212687

First edition 2023

I dedicate this book to my mother, Francisca Edna dos Santos Castro for overcoming her own tragedies with good faith and being the mother I need to have.

ACKNOWLEDGEMENT

I acknowledge my amazing husband, Kazutoshi Yamazaki, and our lovely children Jose and Lucas who have helped me to evolve and better myself. My mother, Francisca Edna dos Santos Castro and my sister Stefani dos Santos Castro Lima Leal, for their emotional support. My mother-in-law, Miyako Yamazaki for her dedication and unconditional love. And also my host-mother Kayoko Kajino for uplifting me and polishing my personal qualities.

PREFACE

Our existence is full of pain and suffering. No single human begin can escape from this fate. However, life can be more and better, we can be more and better. Despite the wounds and scars, life is also, magnificent. The metaphor of a rose and its thorns has been used for a long time in our culture. Both are gorgeous and painful. During these years, especially during COVID, I have been reflecting on these matters. From my own experience, as a kid growing up without a structured family, suffering physical and emotional abuse, having economical distress, infectious diseases, and nutrition deprivation. It is a miracle to overcome all these with sanity. I believe that in part this was possible because I could see the "roses" in my life. I knew the thorns were there, but also that from time to time the magnificence of the roses would come all the disturbance of the thorns.

Memories

All days past
In my sharp best
No days left in my open breast
Petals dancing their final death
My silent rest in your warmest breath
Screaming out
Life is made of simple sounds
Building up or crashing down
Your tender voice makes me sleep
No matter where, how, and why
Mom, life is the wonder of now
You are the best memory in me.

Inside the seed

Can you free a man from his own prison and
shadows?
When his roots are sick and his bark is moldy
There is some hope, there is a ground
There is soil, there is a sound

As trees, man spreads out his leaves on the soil
of illusion
Do not wait for the break and separation,
When the fungus rests free from the destine and
beat a seed

All seeds of yesterday's fruits want to grow
And a Man in a prison let his breath freely in the
air
Craving for a bite of sun and sky
The light that will bring the green
Sadly in his heart is just a weak seed
Fated to never grow, never bloom, never break a
rock
Can you free this man?
Could his splendor nature flourish somehow
Solely a weak seed fighting his primitive base

In a complete lack of sources
Some fresh soil
Some drops of hope
This would be enough.

Last leaf

This winter freezes my brother's heart
In his glasses eyes
My windows watch
Watch the last leaves
Marbles and cheers dance
It is not samba,
It is a sad steps
With beautiful steps
In the air ..
One leaf flies like kids without guide
The winter wind hung her farway
Otherwise the cold flips the molecules
 It may be the cold, or either the road
The cause of my freeze being not dancing too
My stack feet want to go, but they can...
A giant dark ice burnt them all It could be just
me paralytic here
Maybe other season makes life more alive
In the air, on the apples leaves, in the dark ice
and in the liquid love
 The day slide blind to my brother eyes and
 I can see him. So cold breath but still alive
 No more than our dreams in the winter days
I never wished such warm hands on my hands

Or a friendly eyes on my eyes, but today is so
dark and
 I want to break the blocks of ice and walk
 As brave as the sharp wind on the babies face
 As strong as the cold matter on the volcanos
soup
As solid as ice inside my bones I want to be free.
No more shadows sleeping on my muscles
 And I want you too to be free.
Put on your green dress and give me your hands
Thousand of hope invading our souls
And we can lay on the see

Healing (Cura)

In my empty heart
There is no space
No great space
No ever a little tiny corner
For all these dead memories
For these ghost strangers
For those old resentments
For agonic worlds

In my empty heart
The passion for life spill
The great

No meu peito vazio
Não cabe
Não cabe
Não cabe
Estas memórias mortas
Estas feridas purulentas
Estes soluços abafados
Estes gritos não dados
No meu peito derrama
Derrama
Derrama

Derrama
O fogo
Que clama
A esperança
Cresce vivida
Queimando minhas cascas
Estacando minhas feridas.

Everything sleeps

Nothing is our daily bread
Ordinary stories inspire ridiculous news
Like liquid images, spilling across the floor
And the world forgets is time to wake it up

Wake up world
This night is cold
Illusions in the muscle
Forgetting that the truth is there
Beyond filters and software editions
Beyond the neoclassical beauty
In addition to plastic surgery
In the heart of what you call, soul
Your true beauty was there
Flaming the bones without premonition
It was from the broken grains that you made
bread
For your skeletal and smooth fibers, mobilized

And that force that moves you
Beyond yourself
Still hasn't come to pick you up
Lie on an elder's shoulders
To fertilize dreams that don't have a calf
She, at night, gets up and looks at the men

Asleep in the time of any solitude
With open eyes they see darkness

We went heavy in waiting for this force
A drifting muscle
Our wan feet left in the air
What a twist reality
Where will you arrive?
The sick become sovereigns
And the sane servants of insanity
Nietzsche warns us
Of the future kindness underestimation

That force able to move us beyond of ourselves
Still hasn't rest on our shoulders
In this heavy night of August
Our dreams just get up and leave us lonely
Asleep they rust in uncertainty
Waiting for another force
For a fresh night
For our young muscles
For our presence and our hands

The gift

I bring you my empty hands
I don't have gold or flowers
And in my fingers hope slips
Like water, watering the soil to flourish
Maybe a seed of tomorrow
I bring you nothing but my simple words
Here's the only wealth that fit in my heart
Words that will remain in your ears
I bring you my free soul to join yours
Completely and magnetically to yours.

A rose in my heart

The last piece of hope
Remain in hunger
Inside my heart
Craving colours despite the thorns
It is the right size
It is in the right amount
No more no less that my tolerance
Pieces of things past and new
Immaterial but real in a spiritual world
In my tired heart resists
All these greenish leaves
And these passion and pain
More than thorns, roses bloom.

Men rise

Os homens levantam
Levantam nas manhãs claras
mas não enxergam nada
Levantam suas têmporas estreitas e
Na arrogância de sua história
Levantam a discórdia e apobreza

Os homens levantam
Levantam em Agosto
Dias acinzentados e roucos
A poeira, os corpos,
as despetaladas flores de Hiroshima

Os Homens levantam
Levantam o que promove dor
Pois disciplina não rima com amor
E assim
Levantam armas, espadas, canhões, a mão e o
cinto
Mas perdem as guerras travadas em sua própria
alma

Os Homens levantam
Levantam os olhos para o que há de mais alto
E de olhos empinados
Não vêem Deus que está tão perto

Os homens levantam
Levantam tudo de perturbador
Seu status e prestigiado valor
E esquecem que mais valioso
eh levantar
o amor.

Asleep Men

Men woke up
On a glorious morning
But their eyes were still asleep
What they see
Still, they raise temples and churches
Whole cities in blindness
Arrogance about their own history

Men woke up
However still asleep
In these warm brises of August
Gray and hoarse days
The dust, the bodies,
The plucked flowers of Hiroshima

Men woke up
Rise what pain is undoubtedly
As discipline doesn't rhyme with love
And so they raise swords and guns
But no love has been a rise on those days
The wars fought in your own soul
The fights we all fight in silent
None clear our hands

Men woke up
Raise their eyes to the horizon
And with slanted eyes
Don't see the divine inside each man

Men woke up
Raise disturbing actions
Prestigious chaos
Arrogance and delusion
Forgetting what is essential
Burring their treasures
Burning their values
Inside or out they sleep
While their deepest nightmare is alive.

Voices and mirror

Beyond the walls
I hear a voice
Nonstop muttering
Years that froze men's heart
Despite the apathy did not freeze in us

Everything burns when silence comes
And he arrives, sometimes early
With a golden key
Opening the doors of my blindness

Seeing the whole world is too much
So much light does not fit in the iris
Dark velvet of expected solitude
Glass shield guards my abode

Beyond the mirror my voice changes
My silent laughter rests
While the whole world screams
Inside the mirror, lost voices.

The unspoken seed speaks
Reflection of Vanquished Darkness
Yours and my words suffocated
Beat the rocks, beat the hours

In the womb of the earth the inhospitable
conjugations

The roughness of the glass reflected the smile
I find my father's voice
Absent peace translucent man
In the memories of the mirror you collected your
seed
And blew like light into the labyrinths of my
channels

I heard my murmurs tearing in your eyes
Deep and soft eyes, thinking the most sonorous
song
My father, what bitter bread is fruitful absence?
Speak your pain to my astonished eyes
Beyond the glasses
I listen to you
With a love that transcends our faults.

In the World`shoulders

The immobility of muscles embitters my days
And it accumulates at the edges of my wounds
It doesn't use to wait for what's coming
And doesn't have a pulse
Horrible apathy builds this glass screen in my
eyes
And from inside I only watch the world

It was night and hope arrived
Sleeping on the shoulders of the world
I couldn't see the road but little by little I walked
A painful journey full of pauses
Broke me to leave so many framed photos
behind
Starting over from the base with so many broken
things
I wanted to wake up

I wish that the Hope, my best friend, walk it up
But Hope sleeps
What would it be like if she was here
I know the world is strong and has large
shoulders
But I don't know how heavy Hope is
It's not a matter of weight

It is a matter of reciprocity
Walking together, hand in hands
It's overwhelming watching the world
I wanted to move my legs and all my systems
To deserve the Hope that arrives
Even asleep she arrives
On the shoulders of a brave world.

Luta

Eu luto com minhas mãos vazias e o coração
cheio de sentimento
Luto contra minha fragilidade, fraqueza,
ignorância e magoa
Luto como a semente luta com a terra para abrir
suas folhas
E doar algum verde ao mundo tao cheio de cores
cinzentas
E não, não creio que minha luta seja nobre...
Ela carrega a prevenção de transformar o caos
em belo
E isto tem um pouco, senão tudo, da ação divina
Criando o mundo do conturbação do nada
E criou Deus o mundo do caos, fez luz das
trevas, vida da inerte material
Luto com o descaso do espaço que perde suas
linhas e formas
No meio do casa se transborda e convida a
poeira, os fungos e a indiferença
E luto ainda contra a excessiva ordem limitando
o crescimento e a criação
Precisamos dos muros e também de portões
E que vez e outra se abram para fluir ideias,
sentimentos e corpos

Eu luto com minha escuridão e as vezes me
canso
Ate que vejo aquela luz pequenina chamada
esperança
Gritando para minha alma: vamos menina, não
pare, não desista,
Mesmo de vagar continue...
Vale a pena buscar a luz.

Caminhos

Meus passos às vezes trepidantes
Esquecem por que caminham
Esquecem as pedras que encontraram
Esquecem que mesmo solitária não estou
sozinha

Pelo caminho uma mão amiga toca meu ombro
E lembro ...
Lembro que tenho companhia
Por mais profunda e pesada a tristeza
Por mais abandonada que eu pareça
Não estou sozinha.

Às vezes é uma semente germinando
Às vezes é uma flor selvagem abrindo
Às vezes é uma brisa mansa nascendo
Às vezes é um João-de-barro cantando
Ou um desconhecido passando
Seguindo o lado contrário da estrada

Pelo caminho trepidante
Meus passos errantes
Seguem ...
Pelas veredas do sertão de Goiás
Pelas trilhas do Maranhão

Pelas cinzentas estradas do Piauí
Pelas vermelhas estradas do Tocantins
Seguem o destino que ainda envelopado
Grita em minha alma, não desista!
Menina, não desista!

Medida do Amor

Qual o tamanho do amor?
O amor de agora é maior que o de outrora?
Onde deleito meu espírito nestas ondas e
suspiros
Sem compromisso e sem hora
Não sei... só sinto!
Sinto o infinito morando no meu peito
E não tem carne, cor ou cheiro
Uma força, uma paz que move a vida
Sara em mim as chagas e as feridas
O amor de agora e o de outrora não tem medida
Não cabem em mim e transborda
E se une ao mar para habitar o plâncton
E se une ao solo para nutrir as plantas
E se une ao sol para aquecer a vida
O amor de agora vai além do que sinto
Dispensa medidas e simplesmente brilha
Brilha nos olhos
Brilha nos dedos
Brilha nos neurônios
Brilha nos fios de cabelo
Fio, filho, filhos…
Fazem brilhar meu mundo inteiro.

Definições

A vida é o mistério
Ela se faz latente no céu escuro cheio de
estrelas
Nos colapsos celestiais dos distantes planetas
Nos átomos que precipitam sob nossas cabeças
Para compor a essência de tudo!

A vida é um mistério
Ela se desembrulha em nossas mãos
Nos gestos, nas expressões, nos fonemas e nos
versos
Nos textos de nossa história sob as pedras, telas,
livros e novelas
Para amargar a consciência dos homens.

A vida é mistério
Ela se desdobra nas pétalas das rosas
Nos açúcares da seiva que atraem as abelhas
Nos hexágonos da cera que maturam o mel
Para quem sabe, adoçar a vida dos homens.

Refletions

Life is the mystery
It becomes latent in the dark sky full of stars
In the celestial collapses of distant planets
In the atoms that precipitate under our heads
To compose the essence of everything!

Life is a mystery
It unfolds in our hands
In gestures, expressions, phonemes and verses
In the texts of our history under the stones,
canvases, books and arts
To embitter our consciences
To sweeten our sour eyes.

Life is mystery
It unfolds in the petals of roses
In the sap sugars that attract bees
In the hexagons of wax that ripen honey
For those who know, to sweeten men's lives.

O mundo

O mundo é mais que matéria
Mais, muito mais que terras, soluços e pedras
O mundo é mais do que eu, que você e das feras
Ele rodopia pelas galáxias sem pressa
Mais que minhas auguras e durezas
Mais que minha amargura e incertezas
O mundo é mais do que sabemos
Mais vasto que nossa solidão
Mesmo irregular tem um pouco de mar
E ainda duro, não é só dureza
Pela moleza do magma se estreita
Além das formas de se formar
Além de tudo tem espaço pra gente sonhar.

Nas sombras

A noite escurece os homens
E escuros vagam pela vida
Sem direção e sem nome
Pensam que tudo é ferida

Gerações passam
Todas anoitecidas
Turvas neblinas que ressecam a mente
Perdidos na veredas
Caminham com as serpentes
A noite não escurece a vida
Mas os homens desafiam a luz
Bebem, fumam, comem as sombras
Impregnam seu sangue e células
Ficam entorpecidos de trevas
Os homens escurecem a vida
Arrancam o sonho
Abrem as feridas.

Imperativa

A noite escurece os homens
E escuros vagam pela vida
Sem direção e sem nome
Abrem nos outros feridas

Os homens escurecem o dia
Enchendo os olhos de trevas
A luz límpida repudia
Negando sua herança de Eva

O dia luta com os homens
O tempo contra todo os bichos
Numa solidão vaidosa
Sangue que lhe tinge os dentes
Que caminham com as serpentes

Os homens desafiam a luz
Bebendo e fumando as sombras
Impregnam seu sangue e células
Rezam pelas orações incrédulas

Os homens escurecem a vida
Arrancam do núcleo sonho
Abrem no tempo feridas.

Conjecturas

A noite escurece os homens
E escuros vagam pela vida
Sem direção e sem nome
Abrem nos outros feridas

Os homens escurecem o dia
Enchendo os olhos de trevas
A luz límpida repudia
Negando sua herança de Eva

O dia luta com os homens
O tempo contra todo os bichos
Numa solidão vaidosa
Sangue que lhe tinge os dentes
Que caminham com as serpentes

Os homens desafiam a luz
Bebendo e fumando as sombras
Impregnam seu sangue e células
Rezam pelas orações incrédulas

Os homens escurecem a vida
Arrancam do núcleo sonho
Abrem no tempo feridas.

Reborn

I am more than I was
And what I become
In this soft cocoon
A dark and loving voice
In a maternal silence

This loneliness embraces me
So warm and fragrant
With its octopus tentacles
My freedom grabs
There is no suffering
It's easy to stay
Inert to snakes and scorpions
I don't fight, I don't run,
I don't suffer
Sigh… a sharp pain
My hardened shells
And before spring falls
They will fall faster